RON MILLER

JUPITER

WORLDS BEYOND

TWENTY-FIRST CENTURY BOOKS   BROOKFIELD, CONNECTICUT

Dedicated to Chris Miller

Illustrations by Ron Miller. Photographs courtesy of NASA.

Library of Congress Cataloging-in-Publication Data
Miller, Ron, 1947-
Jupiter / by Ron Miller.
p. cm. — (Worlds beyond)
Includes index.
Summary: Chronicles the discovery and explorations of the planet Jupiter and discusses
each of its moons, its place in the solar system, and more.
ISBN 0-7613-2356-2 (lib. bdg.)
1. Jupiter (Planet)—Juvenile literature. [1. Jupiter (Planet)] I. Title.
QB661.M55 2002   523.45—dc21   2001036790

Published by Twenty-First Century Books
A Division of The Millbrook Press, Inc.
2 Old New Milford Road
Brookfield, Connecticut 06804
www.millbrookpress.com

CONTENTS

♃

Astronomical symbol for Jupiter

CHAPTER ONE

THE GIANT PLANET

Everything about Jupiter is *big.* The giant planet is more than 300 times as massive as Earth and 11 times its diameter. It would take more than 1,330 planets the size of Earth to fill a hollow sphere the size of Jupiter. More than twice as massive as all the other planets combined, it is second only to the Sun in its domination of the solar system and about as large as a **gas giant** planet can be. In fact, if more **mass** were added to Jupiter the increased **gravity** would only compress it, leaving the diameter of the planet unchanged. As one astronomer stated, the solar system could be rightly described as consisting of only the Sun, Jupiter, and debris. It is no wonder that Jupiter was named after the king of the Roman gods.

The more massive a planet is—that is, the more material it contains—the greater its pull of gravity. This is why the Moon has less gravity than Earth. Although Jupiter is made mostly of liquid and gas, there is so much of it that Jupiter's gravity is two and a half times that of Earth. A person weighing 100 pounds (45 kilograms) on Earth would weigh two and a half times more on Jupiter, or 250 pounds (113 kg)—that is, if there were any solid place on the planet to stand.

TWO KINDS OF PLANETS

There are two types of planets in our solar system: gas giants, which are made mostly of light elements such as **hydrogen** and helium, and **terrestrial planets**, which are made mostly of rock and metal. Earth is a terrestrial planet (and it gave its name to the category since "terrestrial" comes from the Greek word for "earth"), as are Mars, Venus, and Mercury. Our solar system contains four gas giants: Jupiter, Saturn, Uranus, and Neptune. The four terrestrial planets lie close to the Sun, while the four gas giants lie much farther away. (Pluto, the most distant planet, might seem to be an exception to this because it is not a gas giant, yet it lies very far from the Sun. But scientists believe that it might not be a true planet. Instead, it may be an icy body captured from the vast cloud of similar objects that circle the Sun far beyond the orbit of Pluto.) The two groups of planets took on their differing characteristics during the formation of our solar system. The heavier elements that eventually formed the terrestrial planets were drawn toward the Sun by its gravity, while the lighter elements that formed the gas giants remained farther away.

We are used to seeing a distinct division between an atmosphere, such as our own, and a solid or liquid surface such as land or water. But on Jupiter there are probably no such sharp distinctions. Instead, its atmosphere gets thicker and **denser** as it gets deeper, gradually turning into a liquid, which becomes denser and denser until it finally becomes a solid. At the center of the planet is a relatively tiny core of solid rock and metal not much larger than Earth itself. For practical purposes, it could be said that Jupiter is all atmosphere.

The gas that composes most of Jupiter's bulk is hydrogen, the lightest element and the same gas that was once used to fill balloons and dirigibles. It is a highly flammable gas that combines with oxygen when it burns to form water. (The space shuttle's main engines burn hydrogen and oxygen, so what you see coming out of them during liftoff is steam, not flames.) Hydrogen is the most common element in the universe. Because hydrogen is so light, Jupiter can be so much larger than Earth yet have only 2.5 times the gravity.

Unlike the terrestrial planets, which are all nearly perfect spheres, Jupiter is slightly flattened. The distance from pole to pole is a little less than the planet's width by about one-fifteenth. This is noticeable even when looking at Jupiter through a small telescope. There are two reasons Jupiter isn't spherical. First, it is made almost entirely of gas and liquid. This makes Jupiter much less rigid than the terrestrial planets. Second, Jupiter rotates much faster than Earth does. Its day is barely over 10 hours long, less than half that of Earth's. Since Jupiter is so much bigger than Earth, the speed of movement at its equator is also much greater.

MERCURY VENUS EARTH MARS JUPITER SATURN URANUS NEPTUNE PLUTO

Someone standing on the equator of Earth is moving at about 1,000 miles (1,600 kilometers) an hour, while someone standing (if they could) on Jupiter's equator would be moving at 27,900 miles (44,900 km) an hour! This rapid rotation has not only caused Jupiter to bulge at the equator, but it has a powerful effect on Jupiter's weather as well. It is the reason, for instance, that Jupiter's colorful clouds are stretched into long ribbons around the planet.

A family portrait: the planets and moons of our solar system shown to the same scale as the Sun

CHAPTER TWO

THE BIRTH OF JUPITER

Five billion years ago there was no Sun or solar system. There was only a vast, slowly swirling cloud of dark dust and hydrogen gas. The cloud would probably have stayed this way if nothing happened to disturb it. But something did. No one knows for sure what it was—it could have been the shock wave from an exploding star, for instance—but once the cloud was disturbed it began to collapse. This happened when one part of the cloud became a little bit denser than another part, which caused that part of the cloud to have a slightly greater gravitational pull than the rest. This region began to attract more gas and dust. As that part of the cloud grew denser and denser, it also began to rotate. The more material that gathered in the center, the faster it rotated—just as ice-skaters spin faster as they draw their arms in—and it began to flatten out, forming a broad, thick disk. Meanwhile, the dust and gas in the middle of the disk grew warmer as it was heated by **gravitational compression**. (You can get a sense of this when you use a bicycle pump. As you compress the air in the pump, the pump grows warm.) The denser the center of the disk got, the hotter it became. Soon it became dense enough and hot enough for the hydrogen to "ignite" in a **fusion reaction**. The Sun was born.

But the Sun was not the only lump that formed in the cloud. It just happened to be the largest. There were many others. These circled the infant Sun, continuing to gather material as they did. The available material, however, was not equally distributed throughout the disk. The Sun had an effect on that. The area nearest the Sun had the densest supply. Here the original cloud was thickest, and the gravitational attraction of the Sun was drawing in even more material. The heavier elements, such as iron and silicon, as well as many minerals, were gathering close to the Sun while lighter materials, such as hydrogen and water, remained in the outer parts of the disk.

The area closest to the Sun was too warm for water to freeze as permanent ice. Objects forming there were composed mostly of heavy minerals. These eventually became the terrestrial planets, such as Earth. The area a little farther out was cold enough for permanent ice to form, so the gas giants and their icy moons formed from the vast blizzard of snowflakes that orbited there. Finally, the outermost region of the solar system was cold enough for ice, but there was too little of it to form any very large objects. There we find the home of **comets**, which are little more than giant icebergs. The solar system had itself pretty much all sorted out about 10 million years after it started to form.

Jupiter's composition is dominated by hydrogen and helium. In this way it resembles the Sun, which is also composed almost entirely of hydrogen. In fact, if Jupiter grew only a little bit larger it might have become a star itself, and our solar system would have had two suns. As it is, Jupiter is too small for its gravity to have created enough heat to trigger hydrogen fusion, but large enough that Jupiter radiates more energy than it receives from the Sun. For this reason, Jupiter's weather does not depend on the Sun for its energy—as weather does on Earth—but is instead powered by heat from inside the planet itself.

Because Jupiter formed in a region of the early solar system where there was a great deal of water but not many heavy elements, its moons, at least its four largest ones, are composed mostly of ice. Most of its remaining thirteen moons are probably rocky or metallic asteroids that were captured by Jupiter's powerful gravitational field.

People have been aware of Jupiter's existence since ancient times because it is easily seen from Earth. Jupiter is one of the brightest planets in the night sky, second only to Venus. The ancient sky watchers, however, did not think of planets in the same sense we do today. The word "planet" comes from a Greek word meaning "wanderer," and it originally named a special class of star that seemed to wander among the fixed stars in the sky. Other than that, there was no reason to suspect that the planets were different from any other star.

It was not until the year 1610 that it was discovered that the planets were indeed a very different class. In this year, Galileo Galilei, an Italian scientist, first turned a telescope toward the night sky. The telescope had been invented a few years earlier by someone unknown in the Netherlands. It was considered a very useful instrument for navigators and generals, but no one thought of using it to look at the sky—what would be the point? There was nothing to see but little specks of light. Galileo, never one to take anything for granted, did look. His observations shook the world.

CHAPTER THREE
THE DISCOVERY OF JUPITER

A nineteenth-century engraving of Galileo demonstrating his first telescope

Before 1610, Earth was considered to be unique, with a special place in the universe. Even the Moon was thought to be something very different from Earth—not a place at all in any real, physical sense, but a body made of some perfect material as befitted something existing in the heavens. It seemed to have dark markings on it (the markings that form what we call "the man in the moon"), but these were thought to be merely the reflection of our imperfect planet in the moon's perfect mirrorlike surface. But what Galileo saw through his telescope was a *world*. "From observations of these spots repeated many times," he wrote, "I have been led to the opinion and conviction that the surface of the Moon is not smooth, uniform, and precisely spherical as a great number of philosophers believe it (and the other heavenly bodies) to be, but is uneven, rough, and full of cavities and prominences, being not unlike the face of the Earth, relieved by chains of mountains and deep valleys."

In other words, Earth was *not* unique—there were worlds in space other than our own. When Galileo turned his telescope toward Jupiter he saw that it was not a bright point of light like the other stars, but appeared instead to be a tiny disk with dark bands crossing it. It, too, was obviously a world in its own right. But even more remarkable were the tiny specks of light that appeared near the planet. At first, Galileo thought they were only small stars, but when he looked at them again the next evening they had moved. Galileo realized that these little points of light must be objects circling Jupiter in the same way the planets circle the Sun.

Galileo wrote proudly, "I should disclose and publish to the world the occasion of discovering and observing four planets, never seen from the beginning of the world up to our own times . . . On the seventh day of January in the present year, 1610, in the first hour of the following night, when I was viewing the constellations of the heavens through a telescope, the planet Jupiter presented itself to my view . . . I noticed a circumstance which I had never been able to notice before, namely that three little stars, small but very bright, were near the planet; and although I believed them to belong to a number of the fixed stars, yet they made me somewhat wonder, because they seemed to be arranged exactly in a straight line . . . and to be brighter than the rest of the stars . . . When on January eighth, led by some fatality, I turned again to look at the same part of the heavens, I found a very different state of things, for there were three little stars west of Jupiter, and nearer together than on the previous night." Galileo reasoned that these "three little stars" were the same ones he'd seen the previous night and that they'd changed position by moving around Jupiter.

Jupiter, astonishingly enough, appeared to be not only a planet but one that also had its own moons circling it—three more than Earth did, since Galileo eventually found another one. These moons, named Callisto, Ganymede, Europa, and Io, after four of Jupiter's mythological lovers, have been known ever since as the Galilean moons in honor of Galileo's discovery (although Galileo himself modestly wanted to name them the Medicean planets, after the wealthy Medici family who had helped support his

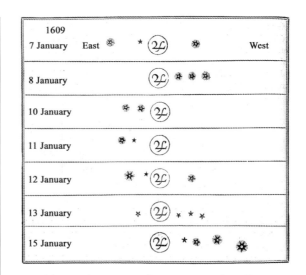

Galileo's drawing of Jupiter and its four largest moons was created in 1610 over the course of several nights. It proved that the moons orbited Jupiter just as Earth orbits the Sun.

Jupiter as it appeared to an astronomer in 1882.

work. Like many artists and scientists of his time, Galileo depended on wealthy patrons to provide him with a living).

Jupiter and its moons were like a model of the solar system. This was one of the most important discoveries of all, because at that time one of the great questions facing astronomers was: Did Earth travel around the Sun along with the other planets or did the entire universe—Sun, planets, and all—travel around Earth? The discovery that Jupiter had moons circling it showed conclusively that not every world in the universe orbited around Earth—and if it was proven that Jupiter had its own moons, then it was proven that Earth was not the center of the universe.

Until twenty years ago not much more information was determined about Jupiter than what could be observed from Earth—and that was very little because the planet is shrouded in a thick layer of clouds. Beyond basic facts such as the planet's size, mass, and temperature, we had to wait until we could send spacecraft to Jupiter to learn what a truly strange world it is.

Until the early twentieth century, most astronomers thought that Jupiter had a solid surface that was probably covered with violently erupting volcanoes. This view of what the surface might look like was published in 1884.

Until the invention of space probes, the only way to learn about a planet was to use a telescope based on Earth. Even though this limited astronomers to what they could see with their own eyes and photograph with cameras, there was still a great deal that could be learned. The size of a planet could be measured directly, and its mass could be calculated from its size and the influence it has on the orbits of its moons. For other information, astronomers could attach special instruments to their telescopes. A device called a **thermocouple** allowed astronomers to take sensitive measurements of the temperature of a planet's surface. With a **spectrograph** a scientist could analyze the light from a planet and determine what elements and compounds exist there. Astronomers also use **radio telescopes** to detect electromagnetic radiation from planets. This can tell them much about a planet's internal structure. Using **radar** beamed from Earth, scientists can map worlds whose surfaces are hidden from telescopes by clouds. Photography allows astronomers to compare any changes in a planet over time—such as the patterns in Jupiter's cloud belts—as well as to enhance details using special filters and other techniques.

CHAPTER FOUR

A MINIATURE SOLAR SYSTEM

Jupiter is a miniature solar system. There are seventeen known moons orbiting the giant planet—and probably many more that have yet to be discovered. Its four largest moons are large enough to be considered planets if they were circling the Sun. Ganymede, in fact, is larger than either Pluto or Mercury.

The first and largest moons were discovered by Galileo in 1610. The smallest and most distant one was found as recently as 1999. This as-yet-unnamed moon is only 4 miles (6 km) in diameter, much smaller than both of Mars's tiny moons. It lies 15,037,880 miles (24,200,000 km) from Jupiter. At this enormous distance even the giant planet looks tiny seen from its moon.

Even though Jupiter's outer moons are only minuscule lumps of rock and ice—none of them larger than 60 miles (97 km) wide—there is a mystery about them. First, they lie in two distinct groups. The inner group of moons orbits at distances between 6,893,000 miles (11 million km) and 7,293,000 miles (12 million km). The ones farthest from Jupiter orbit between 13 million miles (21 million km) and 15 million miles (24 million km).

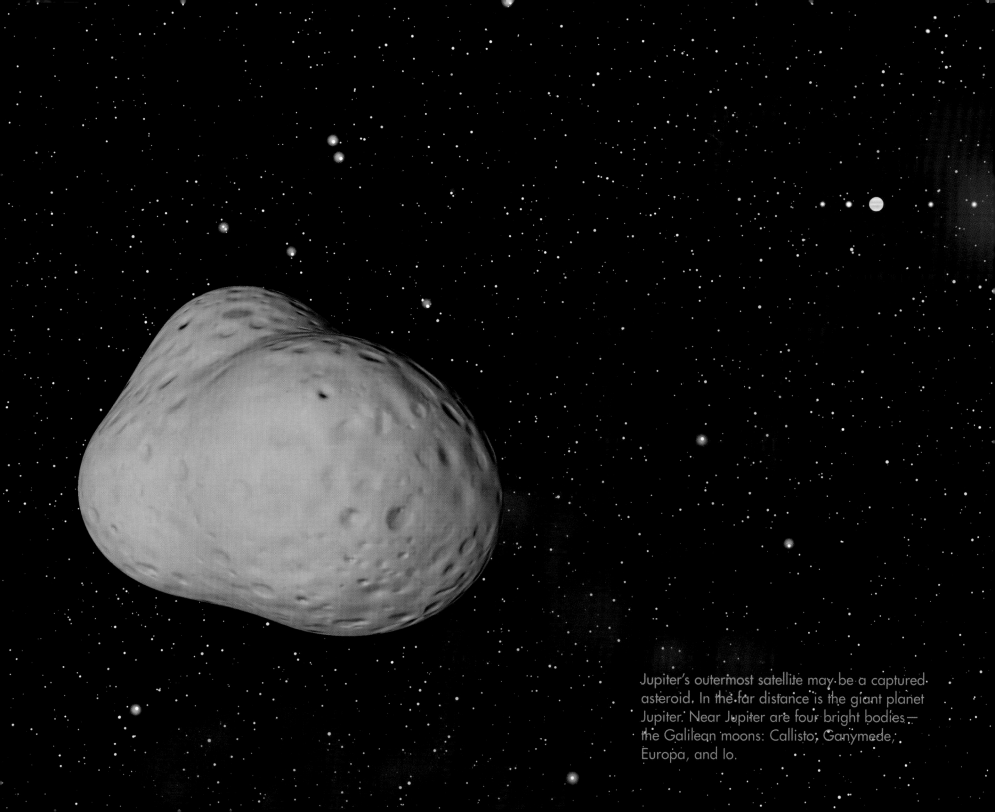

Jupiter's outermost satellite may be a captured asteroid. In the far distance is the giant planet Jupiter. Near Jupiter are four bright bodies— the Galilean moons: Callisto, Ganymede, Europa, and Io.

THE MOONS OF JUPITER

NAME	DATE DISCOVERED	SIZE (DIAMETER)	MEAN DISTANCE FROM CENTER OF JUPITER
Metis	1980	25 mi (40 km)	79,514 mi (127,960 km)
Adrastea	1979	15 x 10 mi (24 x 16 km)*	80,148 mi (128,980 km)
Amalthea	1892	168 x 105 x 96 mi (270 x 170 x 155 km)*	112,660 mi (181,300 km)
Thebe	1980	62 mi (100 km)	137,889 mi (221,900 km)
Io	1610	2,255 mi (3,630 km)	261,982 mi (421,600 km)
Europa	1610	1,945 mi (3,130 km)	416,959 mi (670,887 km)
Ganymede	1610	3,281 mi (5,280 km)	665,520 mi (1,071,000 km)
Callisto	1610	2,985 mi (4,800 km)	1,170,096 mi (1,883,000 km)
Leda	1974	10 mi (16 km)	6,893,812 mi (11,094,000 km)
Himalia	1904	112 mi (180 km)	7,133,672 mi (11,480,000 km)
Lysithea	1938	25 mi (40 km)	7,282,808 mi (11,720,000 km)
Elara	1904	50 mi (80 km)	7,293,372 mi (11,737,000 km)
Ananke	1951	19 mi (30 km)	13,173,680 mi (21,200,000 km)
Carme	1938	27 mi (44 km)	14,043,640 mi (22,600,000 km)
Pasiphae	1908	22 mi (35 km)	14,602,900 mi (23,500,000 km)
Sinope	1914	12 mi (20 km)	14,727,180 mi (23,700,000 km)
1999J17	1999	4 mi (6 km)	15,037,880 mi (24,200,000 km)

*Since this moon is not spherical, its longest and shortest dimensions are given.

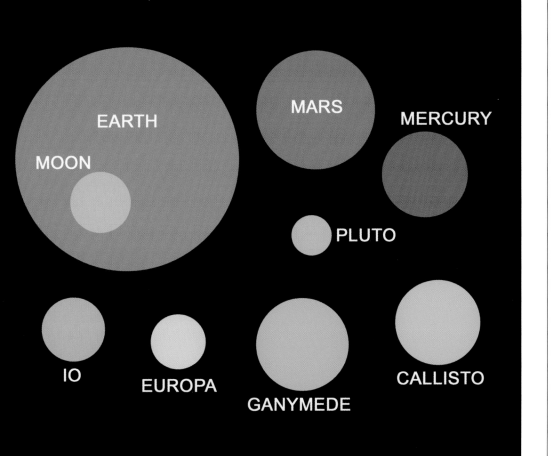

EARTH

MOON

MARS

MERCURY

PLUTO

IO

EUROPA

GANYMEDE

CALLISTO

The four largest moons of Jupiter are among the largest moons in the solar system. One of them, Ganymede, is larger than Mercury and Pluto and only 40 percent smaller than Mars. All but Europa are larger than Earth's moon.

MOONS AND PLANETS

What is the difference between a moon and a planet? A planet is a solid (or partially liquid) body, such as Earth or Jupiter, orbiting a star. A planet gives off no light of its own—it can be seen only by the light it reflects from its sun. A moon is also a solid body—usually made of rock, ice, or a combination of both—that gives off no light of its own. But instead of orbiting a star, a moon orbits a planet. A better word than moon is satellite (which means "companion"). Our moon is the satellite of Earth, while Callisto, Io, Ganymede, and Europa are all satellites of Jupiter. Sometimes they are called natural satellites to distinguish them from artificial ones such as the Hubble Space Telescope or the International Space Station.

All the planets in the solar system and most of the moons are spherical. But many moons (and most **asteroids**) are not round at all. Jupiter's moon Amalthea is shaped like a hockey puck, while the two tiny moons of Mars, Phobos and Deimos, look like potatoes. Large bodies tend to be spherical because the material they're made from is attracted by its own gravity, which pulls them into the shape of a ball. The more material, or mass, there is, the stronger the gravity, and the more spherical the object will become. But an object may be too small for its gravity to overcome the strength of its composition. When this happens, the object can be almost any shape at all.

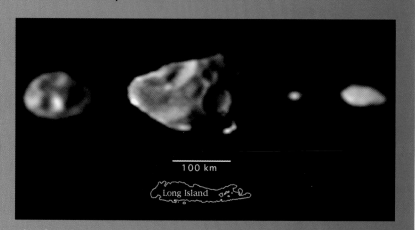

100 km

Long Island

The four small inner moons of Jupiter compared in size, from left to right: Thebe, Amalthea, Adrastea, and Metis. The large crater on Thebe is 25 miles (40 km) wide. The white marks on Amalthea may be outcroppings of ice or material ejected from a crater. (NASA/JPL)

These outermost five moons orbit Jupiter in a clockwise, or **retrograde**, direction—that is, in the opposite direction to all the other moons. Why are the outer moons in two such distinct groups, and why do all five members of one of the groups orbit Jupiter clockwise? The answer to this mystery concerns an aspect of Jupiter that turns out to be very important to Earth.

Jupiter's gravitational field is so powerful that the planet acts as a kind of giant sweeper as it circles the Sun. All sorts of things—asteroids, **meteors**, and comets—are swept up. These and other things could pose a hazard to our planet. In fact, the inner solar system would be a great deal "dirtier" were it not for the influence of Jupiter.

This diagram of the orbits of Jupiter's moons (not to scale) shows that most of the moons orbit counterclockwise (prograde) except for the outer four, which orbit clockwise (retrograde). This may be because the outer moons are the remnants of an asteroid that entered the Jupiter system in a direction opposite to that of the other moons.

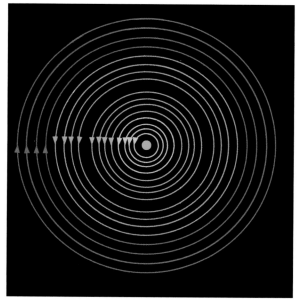

It is known that Jupiter has had many "temporary" satellites—asteroids and comets, for instance, that were drawn into loose orbits around the planet for a short time. The most famous of these was comet Shoemaker-Levy 9, which was attracted to Jupiter in 1993. Jupiter's enormous gravity broke up the comet into numerous smaller pieces that eventually collided with the planet in a series of powerful explosions. This is similar to what may have happened to the outer moons. They may be the remnants of two or more asteroids that came close enough to Jupiter to go into orbit around it. These asteroids may then have broken up, forming the smaller moons we see today. If the five clockwise-

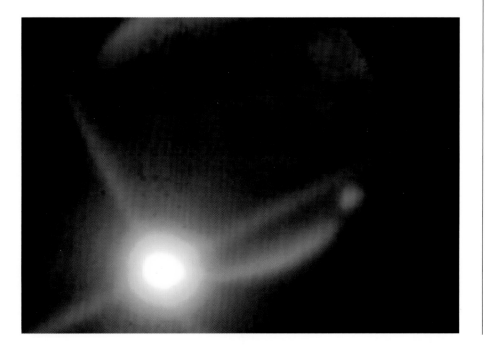

The impact of the fragments of comet Shoemaker-Levy 9 was so violent that the explosions were visible in Earth-based telescopes. (NASA/JPL)

From July 16 to July 24, 1994, fragments of comet Shoemaker-Levy 9 impacted Jupiter in a series of titanic explosions. The comet had been broken into pieces by Jupiter's powerful gravity when it made a close approach two years earlier. Each explosion was as large as Earth itself and exhibited the possibility of what might happen if our own planet collided with a large comet or asteroid. Here we see a comet fragment in the foreground as it hurtles toward Jupiter. Smaller fragments are already hitting the atmosphere and burning up as meteors. In the distance, an explosion hundreds of times larger than one caused by the most powerful atomic bomb erupts in a fireball thousands of miles wide. On the horizon is the dark scar left by an earlier impact.

orbiting moons were a single body at one time it would explain why they are all now orbiting in the same direction—the pieces would continue to orbit in the same direction as the original object. And an asteroid could have entered Jupiter's influence from any direction, which explains why the orbits are "backward." Saturn, Uranus, and Neptune also have small, distant moons with unusual or retrograde orbits that may be captured asteroids.

After the nine tiny outer moons lies the first of Jupiter's giant satellites: Callisto. Like all of the other moons of Jupiter, Callisto is named for one of the many lovers of the amorous Roman god. It is a big moon, 2,985 miles (4,800 km) in diameter, about three-fifths the size of our own moon, slightly larger than Mercury, and the second largest of Jupiter's family. It is one of the original Galilean satellites. About a quarter of its mass seems to be ice, with the remainder being rock and iron. Its surface is composed of dark minerals mixed with about 30 percent to 90 percent ice. There are many **craters** that appear bright white because the impact blew away the darker surface soil, exposing the ice beneath.

Since Callisto is probably composed entirely of a mixture of ice and rock, it does not have the central core that many other large moons and all planets have. This means that it probably never went through a phase where it had a **molten** interior. It is also too far from Jupiter for **tides** to have much effect in heating the moon, as they do for Io and Europa. As might be expected, then, there is a complete lack of any volcanic or **tectonic** features.

Callisto's surface has been heavily cratered by **meteorite** impacts—so heavily, in fact, that no new craters can be formed without destroying old ones. It is the most cratered body in the

Above: Callisto (NASA/JPL) Below: The white rims of many of the craters and ridges on Callisto are bare ice jutting through the surface. (NASA/JPL)

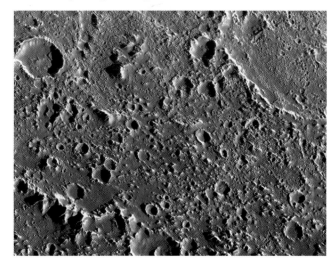

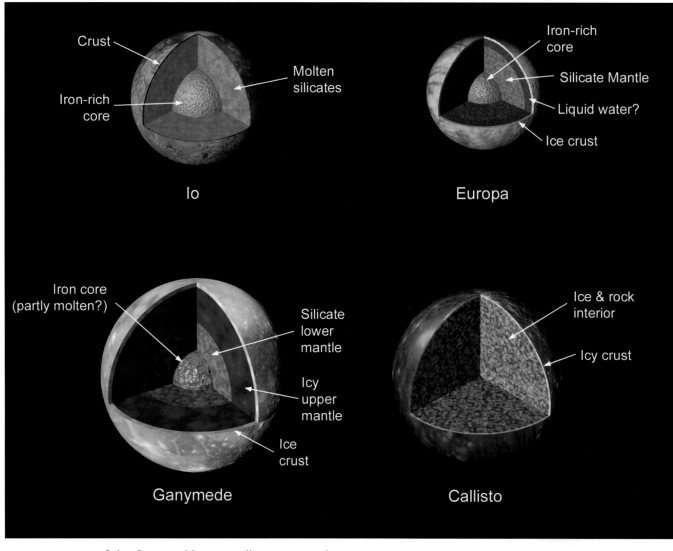

Cross sections of the four Galilean satellites (NASA/JPL)

solar system. One enormous impact feature called Valhalla looks like a series of concentric rings, or a bull's-eye some 1,500 miles (2,400 km) wide. Surrounding it are steep cliffs, or **scarps**. By measuring the number of impact craters, scientists have determined that Callisto's surface may also be one of the oldest in the solar system, having undergone little change other than craters in the last 4 billion years.

Most of Callisto's craters don't look much like those on Earth's moon. Instead, they look flat and shallow. This is probably because the surface is made almost entirely of ice. Over the centuries the surface has "relaxed" and flattened out, flowing slowly under the force of gravity in the same way that a hole scooped out of muddy ground will slowly flatten out. Many craters have

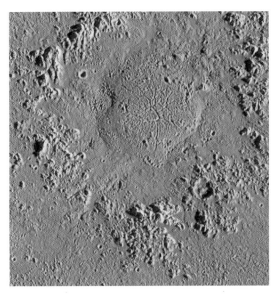

When this large crater was formed, Callisto's icy surface melted, causing its material to splash as when a rock is thrown into mud. (NASA/JPL)

Astronomers can estimate the age of a body such as a moon or planet by studying the craters on its surface. On an erosion-free surface such as Callisto's, impact craters accumulate over time. This allows astronomers to use two different methods to date the age of the surface.

The first simply measures the number of craters. An area that has more craters is older than one with fewer craters, so scientists can get an idea of the relative ages of different regions. Areas that are only lightly cratered, such as regions of Europa and Io, are assumed to be young. This method, however, only gives an impression of the relative age of two areas, but not their actual ages.

The second method can determine the actual age in years. If the rate of cratering is known, then counting the number of craters will give the age of the surface. For instance, if it is known that an average of 10 new craters is formed every year, and a moon has 10,000 craters, it is easy to calculate that the surface of the moon is 1,000 years old. Although the rate of cratering in the solar system involves some guesswork, this method supplies fairly accurate results.

An enormous scarp, or cliff, towers above the cratered landscape of Callisto. It was created when a huge plate of its icy crust shifted.

Giant ice spires tower more than 260 feet (80 m) above the surface of Callisto. The spires are icy but also contain some darker dust. In the distance is Jupiter. The three small dots in a row to the right of it are Io, Europa, and Ganymede. (Also see page 64)

become so flat that only a kind of "ghost" image remains of them. Because these craters have been virtually erased from existence they are called **palimpsests**. (When medieval scribes wanted to reuse a parchment, they would scrape away the earlier writing. These recycled parchments were called palimpsests. There was usually a kind of ghost image remaining of the earlier writing, which reminded scientists of the ghost craters on Callisto.)

Callisto orbits 1,170,096 miles (1,883,000 km) from Jupiter. Although this is nearly five times the distance that separates Earth from the Moon, Jupiter seen from Callisto is so large that it appears more than eight times larger than a full moon does in Earth's sky.

Next in from Callisto, and only 665,520 miles (1,071,000 km) away from Jupiter, is Ganymede. It is not only the largest of Jupiter's moons, it's the largest moon in the solar system. It is larger than either Mercury or Pluto, only 23 percent smaller than Mars, and very different from its neighbor Callisto. While Ganymede's outer surface is also mostly ice—at least 90 percent of it—it has much more rocky material in its overall makeup. A small core of either iron and sulfur or molten iron is surrounded by a deep mantle of rock, on top of which is a relatively thin shell of ice.

The surface of Ganymede also looks very different from that of Callisto. While it has large areas of heavy craters, there are equal areas covered with complex patterns of grooves and ridges. These were probably formed by movement of the ice beneath, much like the patterns found in Arctic ice floes as enormous blocks of ice, moved by the ocean currents beneath them, split apart and collide. The craters of Ganymede are all shallow, like Callisto's, since they were formed in ice, and ice flows under its own weight over long periods of time.

(29)

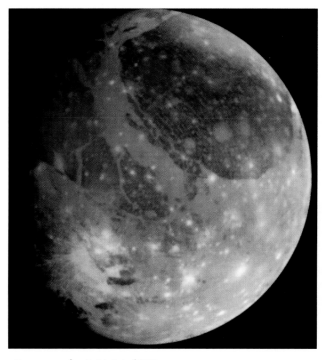

Ganymede (NASA/JPL)

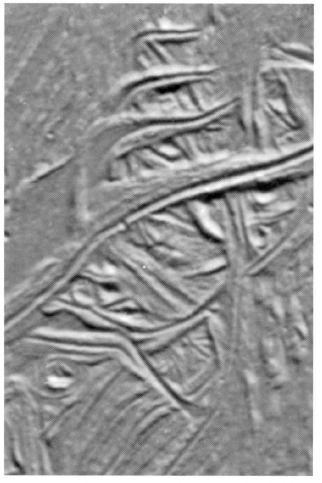

As Ganymede's icy crust shifts, it wrinkles, folds, and fractures. New ice will well up to fill the gaps, resulting in a terrain of complex ridges and grooves. (NASA/JPL)

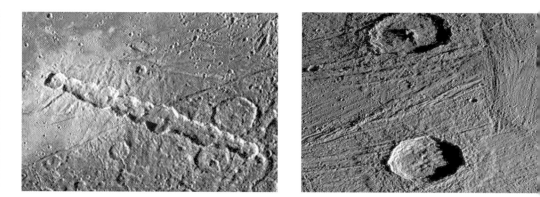

Above left: Enki Catena is a chain of 13 craters that formed when a small comet—probably shattered into pieces by Jupiter's gravity—slammed into Ganymede. (NASA/JPL) Right: Two fresh craters, Gula (top) and Achelous, 24 miles (38 km) and 20 miles (32 km) wide, respectively, on Ganymede (NASA/JPL) Below: A series of scarps in the area of the Nicholson Region on Ganymede are in the form of steps. (NASA/JPL)

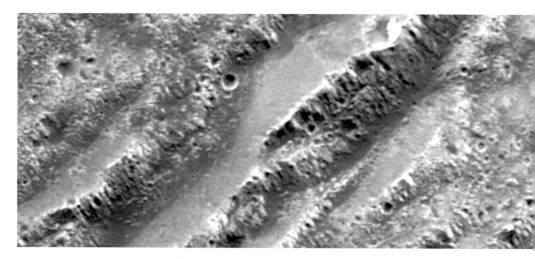

As the icy surface of Ganymede slowly shifts due to the gravitational pull of its own mass, ridges and deep crevasses called rills are formed.

The pressure of ice expanding from below has caused the surface of Ganymede to bulge into a dome called a pingo. These are often seen in the tundra of Canada and Alaska.

Approximately 416,959 miles (670,887 km) from Jupiter lies Europa, the smallest of the Galilean satellites and one of the strangest-looking moons in the solar system. Its surface is covered entirely with complex patterns of overlapping cracks, folds, ridges, and grooves, with almost no craters at all. These features, though, do not rise very high above the surface. In proportion to its size, Europa's surface is extremely smooth, so that it resembles a cracked cue ball more than anything else. In fact, if Europa were reduced to the size of a cue ball it would be smoother than the ball!

This would seem to indicate that Europa's surface is very young—that some forces constantly renew the surface so features are destroyed before they become old. The close resemblance of Europa's surface to the ice floes of the Arctic and Antarctic regions of Earth may offer a clue to what is happening. The visible surface of this moon might be a thick layer of ice floating above an ocean of liquid water. The movement of this ice may cause the ridges and grooves to form, at the same time destroying craters and any other features before they can become very old.

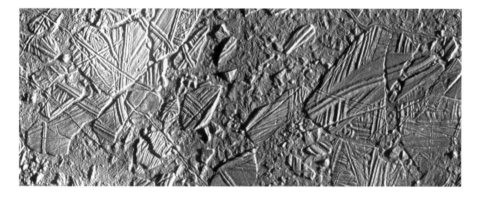

Europa (NASA/JPL)

Left: Ice floes in the Conamara region of Europa: The icy crust is constantly splitting apart while freshwater rises from below and freezes, eventually producing a complicated quilt of patterns. The white and blue areas have been dusted with ice particles, probably from the formation of nearby Pwyll crater, while the brownish areas contain ice that has been contaminated by dust and minerals. The area covered by the photograph is 44 miles by 19 miles (71 by 31 km). (NASA/JPL)

Masses of ice collide on
Europa and create long ridges
that stretch for miles across the
frozen landscape.

Here we see an area on Europa where the ice has cracked apart into blocks, like the ice floes in the Arctic or Antarctic on Earth. Between the floes is frozen water that has been exposed by the moving ice. In the distance is Jupiter, twenty-four times larger than a full moon back on Earth.

Water would also flow up through the cracks and freeze, creating a new, fresh surface. The surface of Europa is constantly being re-created.

The possibility that there may be a vast ocean of water—perhaps as deep as 30 miles (48 km)—beneath the icy crust of Europa is very exciting. This would be the only place in the solar system other than Earth where large amounts of liquid water exist. The water could be kept liquid by the proximity of Europa

As a moon orbits a planet, the planet's gravity pulls on the side of the moon that is closest to it, but pulls less on the side that is farther away. This is because the force of gravity grows less with distance. This uneven pull is called a tide. Tides can cause a moon to flex like a rubber ball. If this flexing is strong enough, it can generate great amounts of heat (it can even tear a moon apart if it orbits too closely). Bend a paper clip back and forth until it breaks and then feel the ends of the broken pieces. They will feel warm. In the same way, the flexing of a moon by tides will cause it to grow warmer.

The heat that keeps the subsurface ocean of Europa liquid and powers much of Io's volcanism comes from the tidal effects of Jupiter's powerful gravity. Io is also caught in a kind of tug-of-war between Jupiter and the large moons Europa and Callisto. Each time the moons pass close to Io, they pull it in the opposite direction from Jupiter. This causes additional stress within Io's crust, generating the extra heat required to power its violent volcanoes.

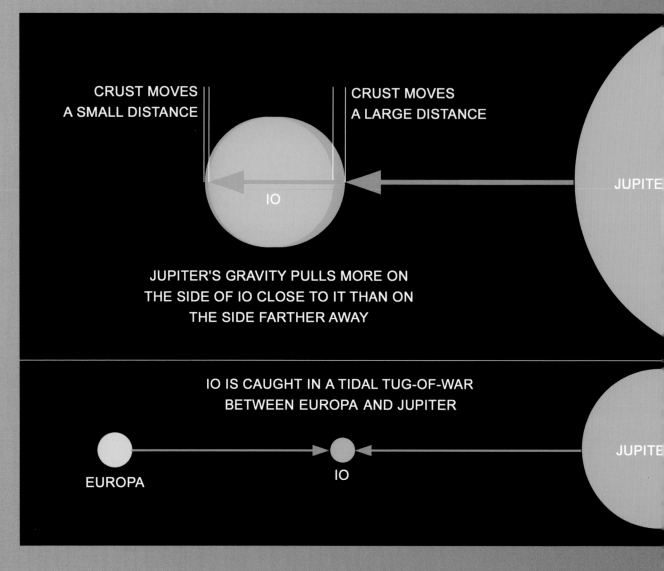

CRUST MOVES
A SMALL DISTANCE

CRUST MOVES
A LARGE DISTANCE

IO

JUPITE

JUPITER'S GRAVITY PULLS MORE ON
THE SIDE OF IO CLOSE TO IT THAN ON
THE SIDE FARTHER AWAY

IO IS CAUGHT IN A TIDAL TUG-OF-WAR
BETWEEN EUROPA AND JUPITER

EUROPA

IO

JUPITE

(36)

to Jupiter. **Tidal forces** from the huge planet are constantly flexing the moon, like a rubber ball being squeezed over and over again in your fist. And just as a rubber ball being flexed this way will grow warmer, the tidal flexing of Europa's crust could be warming the water beneath its surface and keeping it liquid. Because life as we know it requires liquid water in order to exist, Europa might be a good candidate for the search for life elsewhere in our solar system.

Unquestionably the weirdest moon in the solar system is Io, which orbits 261,982 miles (421,600 km) from Jupiter. This is closer than our Moon is to Earth. Jupiter—which is more than forty times wider than our Moon—fills Io's sky like an enormous striped balloon. Io is a large moon, about 2 percent bigger than our own, and unlike Europa, Callisto, or Ganymede, it seems to have little or no ice in its makeup.

At first glance, Io resembles a cheese pizza, with its blotchy, swirling patterns of red, yellow, orange, and white. There are no impact craters—young or old—but instead hundreds of volcanic **calderas**, or large flat-floored craters, many of which are violently active. In fact, there are more volcanoes erupting at any one time on Io than on Earth, making this moon the most volcanically active body in the solar system, with new eruptions breaking out all the time. Some of the most powerful eruptions can throw bright plumes of material up to 186 miles (300 km) above the surface. But these eruptions look nothing like those we see on our planet. Since Io has very little atmosphere, the dust and gas cannot create the billowing clouds we see spewing from volcanoes on Earth.

The plume from an erupting volcano on Io can be seen at the left. (NASA/JPL)

In this panoramic view of Io's surface, one of its flat, mesalike mountains is in the distance to the left. Mountains do not last long on hyperactive Io, and this one is no different. It is slowly slumping and collapsing and will soon disappear, only to be replaced by a new mountain somewhere else. The surrounding surface is buried in debris thrown from nearby volcanoes—mostly rocks and brightly colored sulfur compounds.

Io has a 42-hour day, which is the same amount of time it takes to circle Jupiter. Therefore, where Jupiter is seen from Io, the planet seems to hang motionless in the sky, neither rising nor setting. As Io orbits, Jupiter goes through phases, just as Earth does when seen from our Moon. This series of illustrations shows the course of a single day on Io.

1. The Sun is just coming out from behind Jupiter while the thick atmosphere of the planet is illuminated in a glowing ring, which surrounds the dimly visible dark side. 2. A few hours later, the Sun has moved away from the left side of the view, and the landscape is brightly lit. 3. A little over 10 hours into Io's day, Jupiter is in its first-quarter phase. The brilliant colors of Io's surface glow. 4. Halfway through the day the Sun is behind Io, illuminating the full face of Jupiter. 5. Ten and a half hours later the Sun has set below Io's horizon. Jupiter is in its last-quarter phase. A volcano in the distance has been erupting, and the gases it released into the thin atmosphere are glowing in a brilliant auroral display. Jupiter's own **aurora** is visible as a thin circle of blue light surrounding its pole. 6. Near the end of the day, the Sun is just below the horizon and will soon rise just long enough to pass behind Jupiter again.

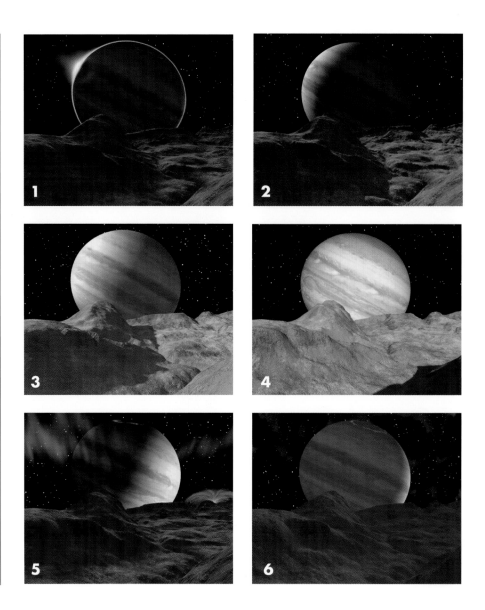

Instead, Io's volcanoes look like vast garden sprinklers, the gas and dust curving in huge arcs, forming umbrella-shaped plumes over the vents. Some of Io's volcanoes spew molten rock, like volcanoes on Earth, while others erupt molten sulfur compounds. It is the sulfur that gives Io its extraordinary colors, since sulfur changes color depending on its temperature.

Since Io is smaller than Earth, its gravity is much less, so some of the material that is thrown into the sky by the volcanoes leaves the moon altogether. This forms a thin cloud that extends all the way around Io's orbit. This doughnut-shaped cloud is invisible from Earth but may be visible from the surface of Io at night, looking something like a glowing yellow aurora.

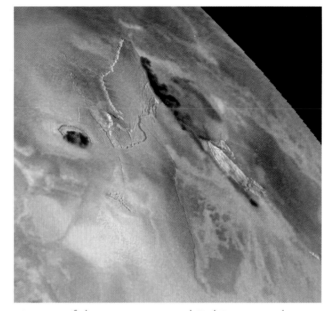

A view of the region around Zal Patera, a large caldera. Io's brilliant colors come from the sulfur that lies everywhere on its surface. Black lava flows have poured from the caldera while bright red material has recently erupted. (NASA/JPL)

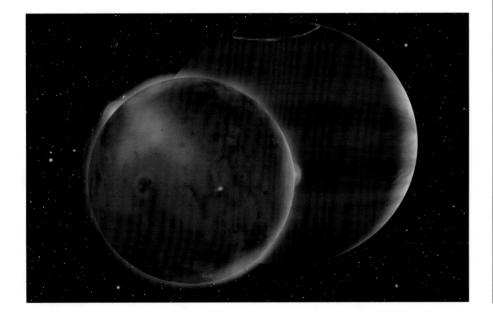

Left: Io's violent nature is apparent in this view of its night side. Powered by the gravitational flexing caused by nearby Jupiter, auroras and volcanoes illuminate the dark hemisphere of the tortured moon.

You would not want to get close to one of the active volcanic vents on Io. It is blasting molten rock and sulfur miles into the sky like a giant geyser. Nearby, a glowing stream of liquid sulfur flows down a shallow gully.

It would be amazing to visit the surface of Io (although the intense radiation that exists this close to Jupiter will probably keep humans away for a long time). There are calderas many miles deep, filled with lakes of boiling sulfur, steaming **fumaroles**, and huge flat-topped mountains slowly melting into the surrounding surface. The landscape is covered with a thick blanket of colorful sulfur compounds that either flowed from the volcanic vents or were deposited from the eruptions.

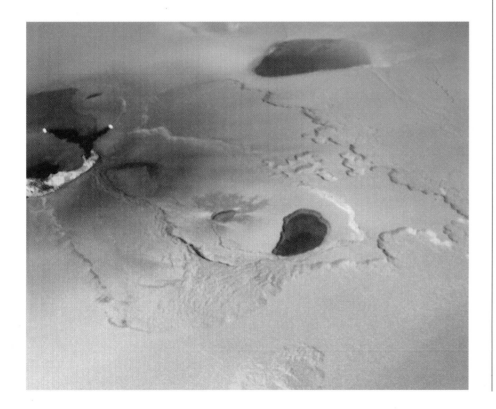

Bright jets of molten lava are being thrown high above the surrounding landscape (upper left) as an eruption takes place in the caldera of Tvashtar Catena on Io. A river of black, molten sulfur is pouring out of the upper side of the caldera, where two bright spots of light mark the exposed ends of the flow. (NASA/JPL)

Several separate photographs were pieced together by NASA to make this full picture of Io's Shamshu Mons, the flat-topped mountain in the lower part of the picture, and Shamshu Patera, the volcanic caldera filled with dark, molten lava at the top. There were no photographs available to fill in the missing black areas on the top and bottom of this image. (NASA/JPL)

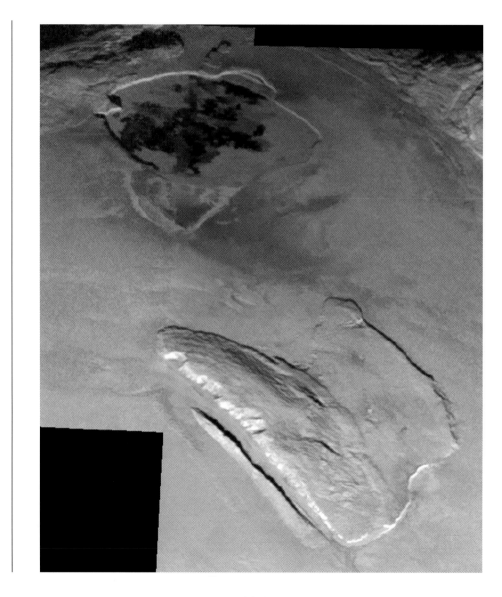

(44)

A lake of liquid sulfur is on the surface of Io. A nearby volcano erupts. The boiling liquid comes from deep within Io's crust, where it has been melted by tidal forces created by Jupiter.

A view of Io from Thebe, one
of Jupiter's inner moons,
shows Io's sulfur dimly glowing. To the right and left of Io
are Europa and Ganymede.

Like Europa, Io's internal heat is created by tidal flexing caused by Jupiter—although since Io is much closer to the big planet its internal tides are more powerful than Europa's. It is also affected by the gravity of Europa and Callisto, as though caught in a tug-of-war between those moons and Jupiter. These forces cause the surface of Io to rise and fall by as much as 330 feet (100 meters) in the forty-three hours it takes to make a single orbit of Jupiter! This movement creates a huge amount of friction within the crust of the moon, which in turn generates vast amounts of heat.

Io is also connected with Jupiter by a **flux tube**—a current of incredibly powerful electricity that is generated as Io passes through Jupiter's radiation belt. This current—5 million **amperes** strong (an ampere is a measure of electrical current; as a comparison, normal household current flows at 20 amperes)—stimulates intense electrical activity in Jupiter's clouds. Jupiter's super lightning bolts are so powerful that they can be detected by instruments on Earth.

Between Io and Jupiter are only a few tiny moons, the largest of which is Amalthea. It is a flattened, potato-shaped object that orbits only 112,660 miles (181,300 km) from Jupiter, which fills half its sky. In fact, from Amalthea Jupiter appears so large that it might be said that it is the sky. Although Amalthea is probably similar to a large rocky asteroid in composition, it is covered with red sulfur deposits blown from the surface of Io by its volcanoes, making Amalthea the reddest body in the solar system. There are one or two bright white streaks on its surface that may be icy rills or perhaps deposits left by meteorite impacts.

Jupiter is seen here from Amalthea. Amalthea is Jupiter's fifth-largest satellite, though it is not very large at all compared to its giant cousins. Amalthea is too small to be spherical. It is 168 miles (270 km) in the widest direction and 96 miles (155 km) in the shortest. Amalthea orbits about half the distance that separates Earth from our Moon, but Jupiter is forty times wider than our Moon, so it fills Amalthea's sky. From this distance we can clearly see the swirling, marblelike cloud patterns and, on the night side of the planet, the glow of huge lightning bolts.

Besides its many moons, a dark, tenuous ring also surrounds Jupiter. It is so thin and dark that no one even suspected it existed until the *Voyager I* spacecraft happened to photograph it when it flew by the planet in 1979. Unlike the bright, icy rings of Saturn, Jupiter's ring is probably composed of dark grains of dust. If you could see it at all, it would be as translucent as smoke from an extinguished candle. Even from Jupiter's ring, which is closer to Jupiter than its moons, the surface of the planet is not visible— there is only a vast, unbroken blanket of clouds stretching as far as we can see.

Facing page: Jupiter's rings were discovered by a lucky fluke. Two of the scientists working on the Voyager mission argued that since the spacecraft had traveled a billion miles, it would be worth checking if any rings were there. Everyone thought that the chance of this was nearly nothing—but when the pictures came in, there they were. Unlike Saturn's spectacular rings, however, Jupiter's are nearly invisible. They are thin, dark, and made of particles of dust instead of ice.

CHAPTER FIVE

JOURNEY TO THE CENTER OF JUPITER

Jupiter is a planet of storms. Vast cyclones rage through its atmosphere. The largest of these hurricanes is so enormous that it is visible from Earth. It was first seen in the seventeenth century, when it was named the Great Red Spot. Its swirling clouds cover an oval about 7,500 miles (12,000 km) wide and 15,500 miles (25,000 km) long—an area large enough to swallow two Earths. The Great Red Spot spins like all hurricanes, but it is so large that it takes six days to make one full rotation. The size and appearance of the Red Spot varies from time to time. There have been some years in which it nearly faded from view. It was at its largest in the 1880s, when it was twice as large as it is now.

Early observers didn't know what to make of the Great Red Spot. Associating its color with heat, some people suggested that it might be a gigantic Jovian volcano. Another theory suggested that it was a huge island of some kind somehow floating in Jupiter's sea of clouds. We now know that the Great Red Spot is a vast hurricane-like storm system. But how can a storm be so large, let alone last for four hundred years? Jupiter does not depend on the Sun to drive its weather, as Earth does.

FACTS ABOUT JUPITER

DIAMETER: 88,850.26 miles (142,986 km)— 11.209 times larger than Earth

MASS: 317.7 times more than Earth

SURFACE GRAVITY AT EQUATOR: 2.36 times greater than Earth

LENGTH OF DAY: 10.66 hours

LENGTH OF YEAR: 11.9 Earth years

DISTANCE FROM SUN: 48,363,562,000 miles (77,831,500,000 km)

The Great Red Spot as photographed by *Voyager 2.* The winds inside this enormous storm system blow in a counterclockwise direction at 250 miles (400 km) an hour. To the lower left of the Red Spot lies one of the smaller storms called a "white spot." (NASA/JPL)

Jupiter does not have a landscape, because it does not have a solid surface. The top of its cloud deck is the "surface" we see from Earth or space. Driven by vast resources of heat from below, billowing storm systems are constantly erupting and swirling into enormous cyclones and hurricanes, some of them larger than Earth itself. The rainbow colors around the Sun are caused by crystals of ammonia ice floating in the atmosphere.

Smaller cyclones—often looking like small white ovals, or white spots, when seen from space—come and go constantly. Occasionally they collide with the Great Red Spot and are absorbed by it, like debris swirling down a drain.

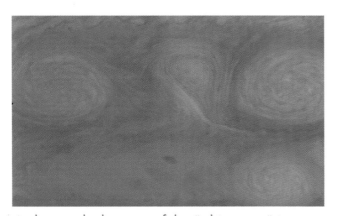

A close-up look at two of the "white spots" in Jupiter's atmosphere reveals their true nature: huge, swirling, cyclonic storms similar to hurricanes on Earth but much larger. The storm on the left is 5,592 miles (9,000 km) wide—two-thirds the size of the Earth. (NASA/JPL)

A hurricane or cyclone on our planet derives its energy from Sun-warmed oceans. When the storm moves over cooler waters or lands, its source of energy is gone and the storm disappears. The temperature changes caused by Earth's seasons also help to create and break up storm systems. But Jupiter does not depend on the Sun for heat. It creates its own. The gravitational compression of its vast bulk generates more energy than it receives from the Sun. As long as that energy source continues to exist there is nothing to keep a storm from stopping once it has started. Jupiter does not have any land to break up storms—the planet is pretty much the same all over. Jupiter also does not have seasons. Seasons are caused by the tilt of a planet's axis of rotation. This tilt causes the amount of sunlight reaching the surface to change during the course of a year. Earth is tilted by about 23 degrees, but Jupiter's axis is tilted by only 3 degrees. This means that the sunlight Jupiter receives is nearly constant year-round.

Over the dark **polar regions** of Jupiter, the night sky is illuminated by spectacular auroras, like the **aurora borealis** on Earth, but much more brilliant and active. Auroras are caused by atomic particles coming from the Sun in a constant stream called the **solar wind**. Because these particles from the Sun are electrically charged, they are attracted toward the magnetic poles of a planet, where they collide with gases in the upper atmosphere. This causes the gases to glow, like the glowing gas in the tube of a neon light. Jupiter has an intensely powerful magnetic field. This not only attracts particles of the solar wind toward the poles—as Earth's **magnetic field** does—it also attracts particles blown off Io, which contribute to the intensity of the aurora.

(54)

Jupiter's powerful magnetic field—ten times as strong as that of Earth—is also responsible for the intense radiation that surrounds the planet. The radiation is due to high-energy particles from the Sun that are trapped by the magnetic field. They form a huge, doughnut-shaped region around the planet where the radiation is 10,000 times greater than in the similar radiation belt that surrounds Earth. It would not only be fatal to human explorers, but it is also dangerous to probes such as *Voyager* and *Galileo*, which must be specially constructed to protect them from the radiation.

The heat that drives Jupiter's weather comes from deep within the planet. The temperature at the core is tremendous—probably about 46,000°F (25,500°C). This heat is carried to the surface by **convection**, much like the heat at the bottom of a pan cooking oatmeal is carried to the top by the churning cereal. When these rising cells of gas reach the upper layers of Jupiter's atmosphere, they are carried off by violent high-velocity winds, stretched into the broad, colored bands we can see from Earth. Differences in temperature and chemical composition create the beautiful colors. The light-colored bands are called **zones**, and the dark ones are called **belts**. The winds blow in opposite directions in adjacent bands, and where the bands shear against one another, complex swirls and loops form in the cloud patterns. Since the colors are affected by temperature, we can tell by its color whether a cloud is low in the atmosphere or high. Blues are the lowest, followed by brown and white. Reddish clouds, like those of the Great Red Spot, are the highest.

In the dense clouds of Jupiter's upper atmosphere, powerful winds blow at up to 335 miles (539 km) per hour at the equator—

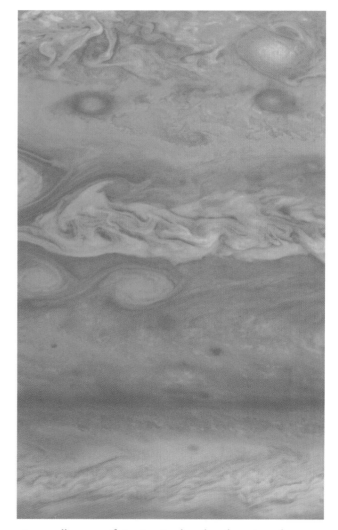

A small area of Jupiter's clouds, showing the complex swirls in their true colors (NASA/JPL)

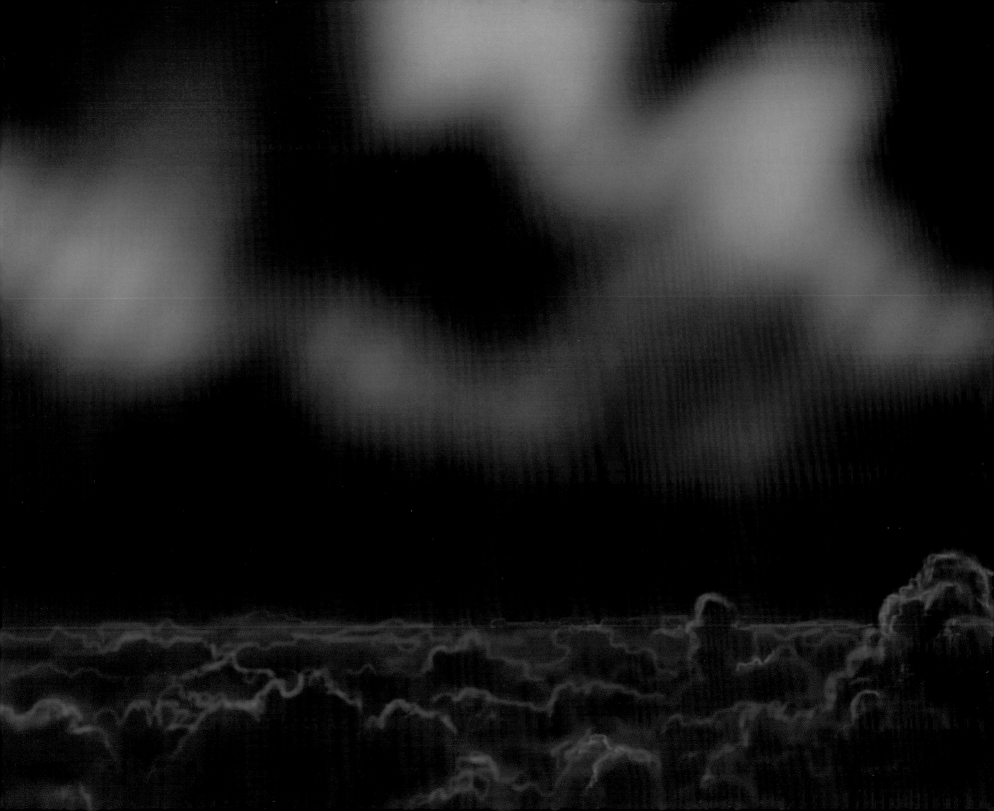

Electrical particles in the solar wind are attracted by Jupiter's powerful magnetic field. When these electrical particles hit the molecules of gas in the atmosphere, they cause them to glow brightly, with different gases causing different colors. This creates a beautiful aurora above Jupiter's poles.

Photographs of lightning were taken in different locations on the night side of Jupiter. Each bolt puts out the energy of 30 million 100-watt lightbulbs—100 times the energy of a large lightning bolt on Earth. (NASA/JPL)

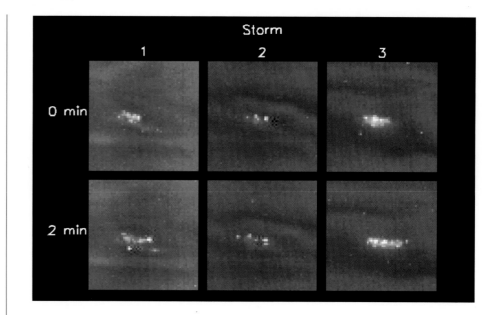

Storm

1   2   3

0 min

2 min

JUPITER THE GENERATOR

Power plants on Earth create electricity by spinning a chunk of metal inside a magnetic field. The machines that do this are called generators. The hydrogen deep within Jupiter is compressed so much that it takes on the electrical characteristics of a metal. This substance is called **metallic hydrogen**. As Jupiter spins on its axis, the liquid metallic hydrogen at its core also spins. This creates enormously powerful electric currents. These are the source of Jupiter's magnetic field.

nearly half the speed of sound. The outside temperature is a frigid −200°F (−128°C). Storms rage all around. Lightning bolts powerful enough to incinerate whole cities flash through the clouds.

Most of the clouds are made of ammonia crystals, ammonium hydrosulfide, and perhaps small amounts of water ice. The cloud deck is only about 30 miles (48 km) thick. Beneath the cloud deck the temperature is almost balmy at 86°F (30°C)—though it would be impossible to enjoy it in an atmosphere of poisonous ammonia compounds.

More than 60 miles (100 km) below the cloud tops is a layer of water ice crystals. Beneath that lies a layer of hydrogen and helium 13,000 miles (20,920 km) deep. To give you some idea

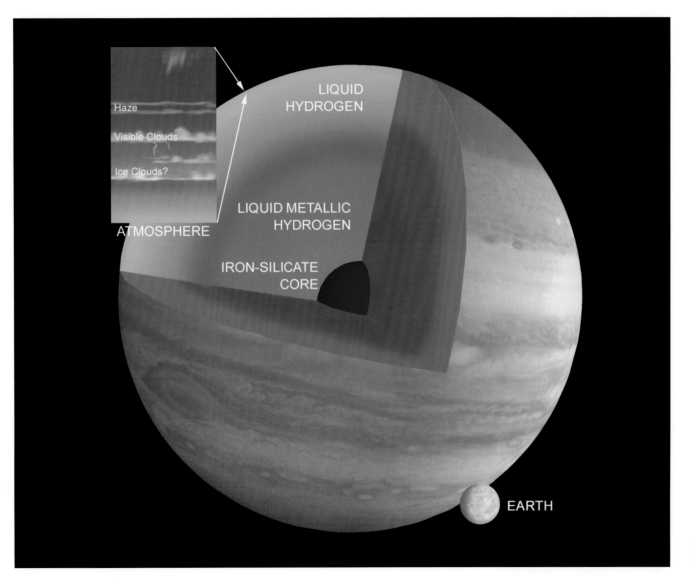

Haze

Visible Clouds

Ice Clouds?

ATMOSPHERE

LIQUID HYDROGEN

LIQUID METALLIC HYDROGEN

IRON-SILICATE CORE

EARTH

A cross section of Jupiter and its atmosphere

(59)

Jupiter is one of the brightest planets when it is visible in the night sky. Whether it can be seen at any particular time depends on where it is in its orbit. Magazines such as *Astronomy* or *Sky & Telescope* can tell you if Jupiter is visible during the current month and where and when you should look for it. The planet is easily visible with a small telescope—it looks like a small yellowish pea with two or more dark bands striping it—and even a good pair of binoculars is capable of resolving the four Galilean moons. *Sky & Telescope* publishes a monthly chart that shows the positions of the four moons for every night of the month, so you can identify which ones you see.

how vast this is, the deepest ocean on Earth is only about 5 miles (8 km) deep. The pressure increases at deeper levels, and the hydrogen gradually changes into a liquid. Unlike water, which has distinct phase changes—that is, intermediary stages between ice, liquid water, and steam—hydrogen gas simply gets denser and thicker until it eventually becomes liquid.

This is still nowhere near the center of Jupiter. Beneath the layer of liquid hydrogen, the pressure increases to an incredible 3 million times the air pressure at the surface of Earth, and the temperature is 18,000°F (10,000°C). Under these conditions, hydrogen acts like a liquid metal. A sea of liquid metallic hydrogen lies 25,000 miles (40,230 km) deep. Earth is less than 8,000 miles (12,870 km) wide—it would be lost in this vast, frigid ocean, like a golf ball dropped into a swimming pool. This metallic form of hydrogen is a good conductor of electricity and the enormous currents surging through it are responsible for creating Jupiter's powerful magnetic field.

At the bottom of the ocean of metallic hydrogen is the core of the planet—the only solid part of Jupiter. The temperature here has reached 55,000°F (30,540°C). This intense heat slowly makes its way back to the surface to drive Jupiter's violent weather. The core itself is probably a sphere of rock and metal only about one and a half times larger than Earth—but the material is packed so densely under the pressure that the core, for all its small size, is ten to thirty times more massive than Earth.

CHAPTER SIX

EXPLORING JUPITER

Until the early 1970s there was no way to explore Jupiter except through a telescope. Yet, important discoveries had been made this way. A great deal of what we know about Jupiter came from the patient observations of hundreds of dedicated astronomers. But Jupiter is very far from Earth—3.5 times farther away than Mars—and even the best telescopes cannot reveal the smaller details. No one knew what the strange Red Spot might be, or what lay beneath the planet's beautiful clouds, or what Jupiter's moons might be like, until the first space probes reached Jupiter.

This happened in 1973 and 1974, when the American probes *Pioneer 10* and *Pioneer 11* flew past Jupiter. The journey of more than 600 million miles (1 billion km) took twenty-one months. The closest approach for *Pioneer 10*, which was launched first, was 81,000 miles (130,350 km), on December 3, 1973. During the two-month-long encounter with Jupiter, the spacecraft took more than 300 close-up photos of the planet, the Great Red Spot, and several of the moons.

Pioneer 11 was launched a year later and made its closest approach in December 1974. The special instruments the spacecraft carried confirmed that Jupiter was made up largely of liquid

This is the discovery photograph that revealed the presence of volcanoes on Io. They were first noticed by Linda Morabito of the Jet Propulsion Laboratory on March 8, 1979. (NASA/JPL)

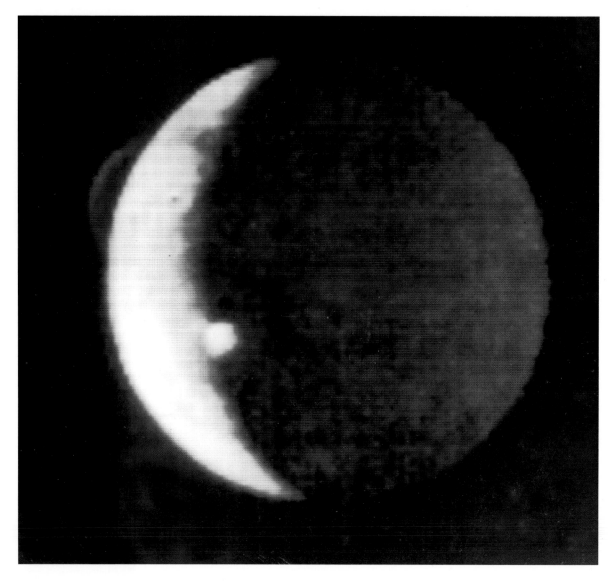

(62)

hydrogen and was without a solid surface. They also measured Jupiter's powerful radiation and magnetic fields.

In 1979, only four months apart, another pair of American spacecraft flew past the giant planet. These were *Voyager 1* and *2* (both went on to explore Saturn; *Voyager 2* reached Uranus and Neptune as well). *Voyager 1* passed within 177,720 miles (286,000 km) of Jupiter and *Voyager 2* came within 400,000 miles (643,720 km). Having much higher-resolution cameras than the *Pioneer* spacecraft, they sent back nearly 30,000 spectacular photos and even discovered four new moons. The incredible detail visible in Jupiter's clouds enabled scientists to deduce much valuable information about how the planet's weather operates. The *Voyager* spacecraft also sent back images of the Galilean satellites, allowing scientists to see for the first time details on the surfaces of Callisto, Ganymede, and Europa. Perhaps the most astonishing discovery made by the *Voyager* probes was the existence of giant volcanoes on Io.

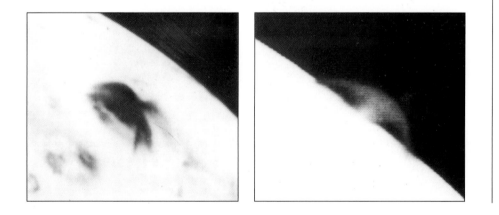

A volcano on Io photographed by the *Voyager* probes: On the left, the plumes are arching out over the surface; on the right is the profile of the eruption, against the blackness of space. Io's eruptions look like this because there is no air to carry the dust and gas being thrown from the volcano, so the material simply travels in a smooth arc instead of billowing in a huge cloud. (NASA/JPL)

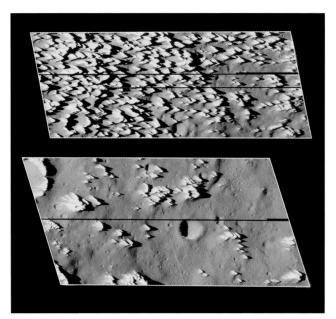

This was one of the last images taken of Callisto by *Galileo*. The strange, knobby spires shown in the upper photo are unlike anything seen before on any of Jupiter's moons. The spires are icy but also contain some darker dust. As the ice erodes, the dark material apparently slides down and collects in low-lying areas. Over time, as the surface continues to erode, the icy knobs will likely disappear, producing a scene similar to that in the lower photo. The knobs are about 260 to 330 feet (80 to 100 meters) tall, and they may consist of material thrown outward from a major impact billions of years ago. (NASA/JPL) (Also see page 28)

The most recent probe, appropriately named *Galileo* in honor of the great scientist who first observed Jupiter through a telescope, arrived at Jupiter in 1995 after a six-year journey. Unlike its predecessors, which zoomed past the planet at high speeds, *Galileo* went into orbit. This enabled it to stay near Jupiter for many years. It has taken thousands of high-resolution images not only of the planet but of several moons as well. It also launched a probe that plunged into Jupiter's atmosphere, where it descended on a parachute 95 miles (153 km) into the clouds. For nearly an hour it sent back information about weather conditions—measuring wind speeds of up to 450 miles (724 km) an hour, for instance—before it descended deep enough to be melted by the intense heat of the lower atmosphere.

EXPLORING JUPITER

SPACECRAFT	DATE LAUNCHED	MISSION
Pioneer 11	April 6, 1973	First close-up photos of Jupiter
Voyager 2	August 20, 1977	Flyby of Jupiter; close-up color photos
Voyager 1	September 5, 1977	Flyby of Jupiter; discovered Jupiter's ring and volcanoes on Io
Galileo	October 18, 1989	Jupiter orbiter and atmosphere probe; close-up photos of the Galilean satellites

Will human beings ever explore Jupiter or its moons? It seems unlikely that Jupiter itself will be visited in the near future: The planet is one of the most hostile environments in the solar system. In addition to the high winds and intense radiation, there is no place to land on a world that has no solid surface. Explorers would have to use a spacecraft that could float high in the atmosphere like a balloon. Even Jupiter's moons might be too dangerous for humans to visit. Io, for example, lies deep within Jupiter's powerful radiation field, which is intense enough to be fatal (it was powerful enough to damage the *Galileo* spacecraft). But history has shown that human curiosity is also a powerful force. As good as our space probes are, astronomers want to see these amazing places with their own eyes. And where humans have wanted to go, they have almost always found a way to get there.

ampere: unit of measurement of the flow of an electric current (named for French physicist André-Marie Ampere).

asteroid: a small rocky or metallic body orbiting the Sun. Usually larger than 300 feet (100 m).

aurora: glowing lights in the upper atmosphere of a planet caused by the solar wind.

aurora borealis: also known as the "Northern Lights," the aurora borealis is the effect of electrical particles from the Sun interacting with molecules of gas in the upper atmosphere of a planet, causing the gas to glow.

belts: the bands of dark clouds on Jupiter.

caldera: a large, often flat-bottomed volcanic crater usually caused by the collapse of the surface.

comet: an ice-rich interplanetary body that, when heated by the Sun in the inner solar system, releases gases that form a bright head and long, diffuse tail.

convection: the circulation of the atmosphere caused by heat.

crater: the hole excavated by the impact of a meteor or asteroid onto a planet or moon.

density: how closely packed the material is in an object; the proportion of mass to volume.

flux tube: a flow of electrical energy connecting a moon and the planet it orbits.

fumarole: a small volcanic vent that releases gas or steam.

fusion reaction: when two atoms combine to create a new element, releasing energy in the process.

gas giant: a large planet

made mostly of gas and liquid, usually with a small rocky core.

gravitational compression: the process by which gravity causes the material at the center of a body to become more densely packed. This compression usually creates heat.

gravity: the force by which all masses attract all other masses.

hydrogen: a gas; the lightest and most common element in the universe.

magnetic field: the electromagnetic field surrounding a magnet.

mass: the amount of material in an object.

metallic hydrogen: hydrogen compressed under such pressure that it becomes a conductor of electricity.

meteor: the streak of light seen in the sky when a meteoroid enters Earth's atmosphere and burns up from friction.

meteorite: a meteoroid that reaches the surface of a planet or moon.

meteoroid: a small rocky or metallic body in space, ranging in size from a grain of sand to a few hundred feet.

molten: state of a substance heated to the point where it becomes liquid.

palimpsest: a crater or other feature that has been nearly erased by geologic forces.

polar regions: the area surrounding the north or south pole of a planet.

radar: from "radio detection and ranging," it is a method for measuring the distance to an object by bouncing radio waves from it and timing how long it takes the waves to return. Radar can also be used to determine the smoothness or roughness of a surface.

radio telescope: a large antenna designed to detect radio emissions from stars and planets.

retrograde: the clockwise movement of a planet or moon as seen from above the North Pole. A counterclockwise movement is called prograde. Most planets rotate and orbit the Sun in a prograde direction.

scarp: a steep cliff created when the land on one side of a fault, or split, in the surface of a moon or planet rises higher than the other side.

solar wind: the stream of electric particles flowing from the Sun.

spectrograph: an instrument that records a photographic image of a spectrum.

tectonic: relating to the movement of continental plates.

terrestrial planet: a planet composed mostly of rocks and metals, such as Earth, Venus, or Mars.

thermocouple: a sensitive device for measuring temperatures of distant objects.

tidal force: the effects of tides on a body.

tide: a bulge raised in a body by the gravitational force of a nearby body.

zones: the bands of light-colored clouds on Jupiter.

Online

Alpha Centauri's Universe
http://www.to-scorpio.com/
index.htm
A good site for basic information about the solar system.

Galileo
http://galileo.jpl.nasa.gov
The official NASA *Galileo* spacecraft Web site.

NASA Spacelink
http://spacelink.msfc.nasa.gov/
index.html
Gateway to many NASA Web sites about the Sun and planets.

Nine Planets
http://www.nineplanets.org
Detailed information about the Sun, the planets, and all the moons, including many photos and useful links to other Web sites.

Planet Orbits
http://www.alcyone.de
A free software program that allows the user to see the positions of all the planets in the solar system at one time.

Planet's Visibility
http://www.alcyone.de
A free software program that allows users to find out when they can see a particular planet and where to look for it in the sky.

Solar System Simulator
http://space.jpl.nasa.gov/
An amazing Web site that allows the visitor to travel to all the planets and moons and create their own views of these distant worlds.

Books

Beatty, J. Kelly, Carolyn Collins Petersen, and Andrew Chaikin, eds. *The New Solar System.* Cambridge, MA: Sky Publishing Corp, 1999.

Hartmann, William K. *Moons and Planets.* Belmont, CA: Wadsworth Publishing, 1999.

Kallen, Stuart A. *Exploring the Origins of the Universe.* Brookfield, CT: Twenty-First Century Books, 1997.

Miller, Ron, and William K. Hartmann. *The Grand Tour.* New York: Workman Publishing, 1993.

Scagell, Robine. *The New Book of Space.* Brookfield, CT: Copper Beech, 1997.

Spangenburg, Ray, and Kit Moser. *A Look at Jupiter.* Danbury, CT: Franklin Watts, 2001.

———. *Artificial Satellites.* Danbury, CT: Franklin Watts, 2001.

Vogt, Gregory L. *Deep Space Astronomy.* Brookfield, CT: Twenty-First Century Books, 1999.

———. *Disasters in Space Exploration.* Brookfield, CT: The Millbrook Press, 2001.

Magazines

Astronomy
http://www.astronomy.com

Sky & Telescope
http://www.skypub.com

Organizations

American Astronomical Society
2000 Florida Avenue NW
Suite 400
Washington, DC 20009-1231
http://www.AAS.org

Association of Lunar and Planetary Observers
PO Box 171302
Memphis, TN 38187-1302
http://www.lpl.arizona.edu/alpo/

Astronomical Society of the Pacific
390 Ashton Avenue
San Francisco, CA 94112
http://www.aspsky.org

The Planetary Society
65 N. Catalina Avenue
Pasadena, CA 91106
http://planetary.org